# Mandalas
## Coloring Book

Jessica Mazurkiewicz

DOVER PUBLICATIONS, INC.
Mineola, New York

This beautiful coloring collection features thirty exquisite mandala designs—each one a collage of interlocking and overlapping geometric shapes, spirals, swirls, and other motifs. Detailed designs are perfect for the enthusiastic colorist, plus perforated pages make displaying finished work easy!

*Copyright*

Copyright © 2015 by Dover Publications, Inc.
All rights reserved.

*Bibliographical Note*

*Mandalas Coloring Book* is a new work first published by Dover Publications, Inc., in 2015.

*International Standard Book Number*

ISBN-13: 978-0-486-80214-5
ISBN-10: 0-486-80214-0

Manufactured in the United States by RR Donnelley
80214006    2015
www.doverpublications.com

# Draw Your Own Mandalas Design